POWER SNACKS

POWER SNACKS

50 SUPER HEALTHY SNACKS

PACKED WITH NUTRIENTS

LOVE FOOD™

This edition published by Parragon Books Ltd in 2015
LOVE FOOD is an imprint of Parragon Books Ltd

Parragon Books Ltd
Chartist House
15–17 Trim Street
Bath BA1 1HA, UK
www.parragon.com/lovefood

ISBN 978-1-4723-7595-7

Printed in China

Project managed by Andrea O'Connor
Designed by Persephone Coelho
New recipes by Sara Lewis
New photography by Ian Garlick
Edited by Fiona Biggs

Notes for the Reader

This book uses both metric and imperial measurements. Follow the same units of measurement throughout; do not mix metric and imperial. All spoon measurements are level: teaspoons are assumed to be 5 ml, and tablespoons are assumed to be 15 ml. Unless otherwise stated, milk is assumed to be full fat, eggs and individual vegetables are medium, and pepper is freshly ground black pepper. Unless otherwise stated, all root vegetables should be peeled prior to using.

Garnishes, decorations and serving suggestions are all optional and not necessarily included in the recipe ingredients or method. Any optional ingredients and seasoning to taste are not included in the nutritional analysis. The times given are an approximate guide only. Preparation times differ according to the techniques used by different people and the cooking times may also vary from those given. Optional ingredients, variations or serving suggestions have not been included in the time calculations.

While the author has made all reasonable efforts to ensure that the information contained in this book is accurate and up to date at the time of publication, anyone reading this book should note the following important points:

Medical and pharmaceutical knowledge is constantly changing and the author and the publisher cannot and do not guarantee the accuracy or appropriateness of the contents of this book;

In any event, this book is not intended to be, and should not be relied upon, as a substitute for appropriate, tailored professional advice. Both the author and the publisher strongly recommend that a doctor or other healthcare professional is consulted before embarking on major dietary changes;

For the reasons set out above, and to the fullest extent permitted by law, the author and publisher: (i) cannot and do not accept any legal duty of care or responsibility in relation to the accuracy or appropriateness of the contents of this book, even where expressed as 'advice' or using other words to this effect; and (ii) disclaim any liability, loss, damage or risk that may be claimed or incurred as a consequence – directly or indirectly – of the use and/or application of any of the contents of this book.

CONTENTS

INTRODUCTION

Do you often find yourself feeling like you're "running on empty" in the middle of the afternoon, desperate for a snack to help you keep going? While a slice of cake or chocolate bar might seem like an obvious choice for a quick boost, they soon make your energy levels plummet and can leave you feeling even more exhausted than before.

To fuel our bodies effectively – without the rollercoaster of highs and lows – we need good-quality protein, healthy fats, some carbohydrates and lots of vegetables. Choosing snacks that are nutrient-dense, rich in superfoods and made with smart, complex carbs will mean you are able to stay full for longer. Wholegrain nuts, seeds, meat, fruit and vegetables all form a good foundation for healthy snacks, and you don't even need to give up the chocolate completely – just be sure to choose plain chocolate with a minimum of 70% cocoa solids instead of the sugar-laden milk chocolate varieties.

Obesity levels are steadily rising and the central culprit is the amount of sugar and processed ingredients in our diet. While we might all love a drive-through snack of burger and chips or a sugary doughnut, they are full of empty calories, saturated fats, and highly-processed sugars and salt, which offer little to no nutritional value.

Have you ever looked at the ingredients list on the back of your favourite shop-bought snack? In addition to the main ingredient, a host of sweeteners, flavourings and additives are likely to follow, with ingredients you have probably never heard of included to prolong the shelf life. These chemical nasties in our food are quickly forgotten when we're reaching for a cookie at 4 p.m., but you can avoid them completely by preparing your own nutritious and sustainable power snacks.

Made with simple, readily available ingredients, home-made power snacks can be prepared with minimal fuss and expense. Source raw ingredients from your local farmers' market, supermarket and health food store to create delicious snacks packed with essential vitamins, minerals, protein and good fats.

Complex carbs are great for filling a hole between meals – they take longer for the body to digest and help stabilize blood sugar to keep you on an even keel throughout the day without the crashes and cravings.

Choose from porridge oats, popcorn, quinoa, wholegrain rice, sweet potato or pumpkin. The other essential ingredient in feeling full is protein – and you needn't eat a large steak to get it. Nuts and seeds are great protein sources too and are easy to transport and graze on when out and about.

When it comes to fat, it's important to make the distinction between the harmful trans fats found in fried, fast and processed food, and natural and intensely healthy fats. Not only are these good for you, but you cannot survive without them as they contain essential fatty acids that aid the absorption of important fat-soluble vitamins, such as A, D, E and K. These fats include ingredients like full-fat milk and cheese, butter, oily fish, olive oil, and nuts and seeds. They might register quite high on a calorie count, but they are healthy fats and this is the important bit. Focusing more on the nutritional profile of foods instead of their caloric status allows us to eat the whole and natural ingredients our bodies need for optimum health.

We should all be eating a minimum of five portions of fruit and vegetables a day, but some statistics suggest that not enough of us are reaching this target. Sneaking them into snacks is a great way to ensure you're getting the recommended amount (and more!) of these essential foods. And you needn't rely on a simple apple or carrot stick to meet your quota by using fruit and vegetables as the foundation of your power snacks, you can ensure you get a good dose throughout the day.

In this book you will find a wide range of fresh, natural and super-healthy snacks to choose from. An 'On the Go' chapter contains delicious snacks to carry with you while you're out and about, meaning you'll be less tempted by fast-food alternatives. A whole chapter on 'Take to Work' snacks has the office covered as well, with a variety of sweet and savoury bites to have on hand when the 4 p.m. sugar-dip hits. 'High Energy' includes high-protein, energy-boosting suggestions for snacks, ideal for pre- and post-workout. Designed for days when you have a little more time to prepare, the 'Weekend Snacks' chapter includes mouth-watering snacks to be enjoyed at leisure, while the 'Sweet Indulgence' chapter offers a go-to collection of recipes for any sugary taste or craving.

Designed to change the way you snack and fuel your body for long-term health and vitality, these power-packed snacks will leave you feeling full, satisfied and, above all, well nourished.

1

ON THE GO

Like to have a few snacks on you when you're out and about? This chapter includes an array of delicious and easily portable snacks for eating on the go.

GRAPE & LYCHEE REVIVER JUICE

The combination of fragrant lychees and creamy avocado in this juice make it the perfect pick-me-up to rehydrate and fight fatigue.

SERVES: 1   PREP: 10–15 MINS   CHILL: NO CHILLING

300 g/10½ oz green grapes

55 g/2 oz young spinach

½ ripe avocado, stoned and flesh scooped from the skin, plus a slice to serve (optional)

5 lychees, peeled and pitted

small handful of crushed ice

125 ml/4 fl oz chilled water

1. Feed the grapes and spinach through a juicer.

2. Pour the juice into a blender, add the avocado, lychees and crushed ice, and process until smooth.

3. Add the water and process again.

4. Pour into a glass, add the avocado slice (if using) and serve immediately.

10

per serving: 413 kcals / 15.6g fat
2.1g sat fat / 72.8g carbs / 54.6g sugars
0.1g salt / 11.2g fibre / 6.3g protein

SPICE-ROASTED EDAMAME & CRANBERRIES

Frozen edamame or young soya beans make a healthy, protein-packed snack and their high levels of fibre keep you feeling fuller, longer.

SERVES: 4   **PREP: 15 MINS, PLUS COOLING**   **COOK: 15 MINS**

350 g/12 oz frozen edamame (green soya) beans

5-cm/2-inch piece fresh ginger, peeled and finely grated

1 tsp Sichuan peppercorns, roughly crushed

1 tbsp soy sauce

1 tbsp olive oil

3 small star anise

40 g/1½ oz dried cranberries

per serving: 179 kcals / 9.1g fat
1g sat fat / 12.2g carbs / 7.3g sugars
0.5g salt / 4.3g fibre / 11.1g protein

1. Preheat the oven to 180°C/350°F/Gas Mark 4. Place the beans in a roasting tin, then sprinkle over the ginger and peppercorns, drizzle with soy sauce and oil, and mix together.

2. Tuck the star anise in among the beans, then roast, uncovered, in the preheated oven for 15 minutes.

3. Stir in the cranberries and leave to cool. Spoon into a small jar and eat within 12 hours.

12

TOP TIP

Edamame beans are extremely versatile and pack a much greater nutritional punch than frozen peas.

PUMPKIN & PEPITA MUFFINS

With just a hint of sweetness, these gingery muffins taste delicious still warm from the oven with a generous spreading of butter.

MAKES: 12   PREP: 25–30 MINS, PLUS COOLING   COOK: 30 MINS

light olive oil, for oiling
250 g/9 oz peeled, deseeded pumpkin, cut into 1-cm/½-inch dice
4-cm/1½-inch piece fresh ginger, scrubbed and coarsely grated
3 eggs
4 tbsp maple syrup
225 ml/8 fl oz low-fat natural yogurt
150 g/5½ oz wholemeal flour
100 g/3½ oz fine cornmeal
3 tsp baking powder
1 tsp ground mixed spice
3 tbsp pepita (pumpkin) seeds

per muffin: 144 kcals / 3.7g fat
1g sat fat / 23.3g carbs / 5.8g sugars
0.9g salt / 1.6g fibre / 5.7g protein

1. Preheat the oven to 190°C/375°F/Gas Mark 5. Lightly brush a 12-hole muffin tin with oil.

2. Place the pumpkin in the top of a steamer set over a saucepan of gently simmering water, cover and cook for 15 minutes, until just soft. Mash and mix with the grated ginger.

3. Place the eggs, maple syrup and yogurt in a medium-sized bowl and whisk together.

4. Put the flour, cornmeal, baking powder and mixed spice into a larger bowl and stir together, then add the mashed pumpkin and egg mix, and briefly whisk together until just combined.

5. Spoon the batter into the prepared tin, sprinkle the tops with the seeds, then bake in the preheated oven for 15 minutes, until well risen and golden brown. Leave to cool in the tin for 5 minutes, then loosen the edges with a knife, turn out onto a wire rack and leave to cool completely. These are best eaten within 2 days of making.

MIXED QUINOA BALLS

One recipe, three flavours – these super-powered balls are a great get-ahead snack. Cook up a big batch to carry on the go.

MAKES: 24   **PREP: 35 MINS, PLUS CHILLING**   **COOK: 35 MINS**

115 g/4 oz quinoa
350 ml/12 fl oz boiling water
3 tomatoes, halved
2 garlic cloves, finely chopped
2 tsp torn fresh thyme leaves
2 tbsp virgin olive oil
115 g/4 oz young spinach leaves, rinsed and drained
175 g/6 oz feta cheese, drained weight, finely grated
pinch of grated nutmeg
25 g/1 oz stoned black olives, finely chopped
1 tbsp chopped fresh basil
sea salt and pepper
sweet chilli jam, to serve (optional)

per ball: 52 kcals / 3.1g fat
1.3g sat fat / 4.3g carbs / 0.8g sugars
0.3g salt / 1.9g fibre / 2g protein

1. Add the quinoa and water to a medium-sized saucepan, cover and cook over a medium heat for about 20 minutes, stirring occasionally, until the quinoa is soft and has absorbed all the water.

2. Meanwhile, preheat the grill. Arrange the tomatoes, cut-side up, on the base of a foil-lined grill rack. Sprinkle with the garlic, thyme and a little salt and pepper, then drizzle with 1 tablespoon of the oil and grill for 10 minutes.

3. Add the spinach to a dry, non-stick frying pan and cook for 2–3 minutes, until just wilted. Scoop out of the pan and finely chop, then mix with one third of the quinoa, one third of the cheese, a little nutmeg, and salt and pepper to taste.

4. Peel the tomatoes, chop and add with any pan juices to the empty spinach pan. Stir in half the remaining quinoa and cook for 2–3 minutes, until the mixture is dry enough to shape into a ball. Remove from the heat and stir in half the remaining cheese.

5. Mix the remaining quinoa and cheese with the olives, basil and a little salt and pepper. Shape each of the flavoured quinoa mixtures into 8 small balls. Chill until ready to serve.

6. Preheat the oven to 180°C/350°F/Gas Mark 4. Brush a roasting tin with the remaining oil, add the quinoa balls and bake for 10 minutes, turning once, until the edges are golden brown and the cheese has melted. Serve hot or cold with sweet chilli jam, if using, for dipping. Transfer the cooled quinoa balls to an airtight container, refrigerate and eat within 2–3 days.

MIXED NUTS IN HERBED SALT

Simple to make and wonderfully tasty, these moreish pan-roasted nuts are bursting with protein, healthy fats and lots of flavour.

SERVES: 4   PREP: 10 MINS, PLUS COOLING   COOK: 5 MINS

1 tbsp olive oil

2 fresh rosemary sprigs, leaves torn from the stems

55 g/2 oz cashew nuts

55 g/2 oz pecan nuts

55 g/2 oz unblanched almonds

55 g/2 oz unblanched hazelnuts

½ tsp sea salt

per serving: 366 kcals / 34.4g fat
3.5g sat fat / 11.3g carbs / 2.5g sugars
0.7g salt / 4.8g fibre / 8.7g protein

1. Heat the oil and rosemary in a medium frying pan, then swirl the oil around the pan to infuse with the rosemary. Add the nuts and cook over a medium heat for 2–3 minutes, until lightly toasted.

2. Stir in the salt, then spoon the nuts into a bowl and leave to cool before eating. Any leftover nuts can be stored in the refrigerator in a plastic container or preserving jar for up to 3 days.

19

SPICE IT UP

Instead of rosemary, try replacing with a little curry powder or a blend of ground turmeric, garam masala, smoked paprika and a pinch of chilli.

On the go

EDAMAME

A common ingredient in Japanese cuisine, edamame beans are the immature green soya beans still in the pod. Typically, the beans are boiled and served with salt.

LYCHEES

Lychees are a subtropical fruit native to China. They feature significantly in traditional Chinese medicine as all parts of the fruit, including its flesh, seeds, bark, root and flowers have health benefits.

BEETROOT

The earthy sweetness of beetroot and its impressive nutritients have increased its popularity over the years. Don't overlook the beetroot greens either – they can be cooked the same way as spinach.

PUMPKIN SEEDS

Containing high amounts of zinc and magnesium, pumpkin seeds are one of the most versatile superfoods you can incorporate into your diet.

APRICOTS

Like peaches and plums, apricots are members of the rose family. They are rich in vitamin A and a good source of vitamin C, potassium and dietary fibre.

ALMONDS

Bursting with healthy fats and protein, almonds are among the most valuable superfoods. Choose almonds with the skins on (instead of blanched) as these contain the highest concentration of nutrients.

ROOT VEGETABLE CRISPS WITH HERBY YOGURT DIP

Making your own crisps is surprisingly easy and you can be certain there are no added artificial flavourings or preservatives.

SERVES: 4   PREP: 30–35 MINS, PLUS COOLING   COOK: 12–16 MINS

1 kg/2 lb 4 oz mixed root vegetables, such as carrots, parsnips, sweet potatoes or golden beetroot, very thinly sliced

4 tbsp virgin olive oil

sea salt and pepper

HERBY YOGURT DIP

200 g/7 oz Greek-style natural yogurt

2 garlic cloves, finely chopped

4 tbsp finely chopped fresh herbs, such as flat-leaf parsley, chives, basil or oregano

per serving: 320 kcals / 9.6g fat
1.1g sat fat / 37.7g carbs / 14.7g sugars
1.8g salt / 8.4g fibre / 7.8g protein

1. Preheat the oven to 200°C/400°F/Gas Mark 6. To make the herby yogurt dip, spoon the yogurt into a small bowl, then stir in the garlic and herbs, and season with salt and pepper. Cover and chill in the refrigerator until ready to serve.

2. Put the vegetables in a large bowl. Slowly drizzle over the oil, gently turning the vegetables as you go, until they are thoroughly coated.

3. Arrange the vegetables over three baking sheets in a single layer, then season with salt and pepper. Bake for 8–10 minutes, then check – the slices in the corners of the trays will cook more quickly, so transfer any that are crisp and golden to a wire rack. Cook the rest for 2–3 minutes more, then transfer any more cooked crisps to the wire rack. Cook the remaining slices for 2–3 minutes more if needed, then transfer any remaining crisps to the wire rack and leave to cool.

4. Arrange the crisps in a bowl and spoon the dip into a smaller bowl to serve. Any leftover crisps can be stored in an airtight container for up to 2 days.

22

SMOKY PAPRIKA ROASTED CHICKPEAS

Chickpeas are made up of complex carbohydrates, which take longer for the body to digest and so give a slower release of energy.

SERVES: 4   PREP: 15 MINS, PLUS COOLING   COOK: 18–24 MINS

2 tbsp olive oil
1 tsp cumin seeds, roughly crushed
1 tsp smoked mild paprika
¼ tsp ground allspice
¼ tsp ground cinnamon
½ tsp sea salt
800 g/1 lb 12 oz canned chickpeas in water, drained
2 tbsp date syrup

per serving: 235 kcals / 8.3g fat
1g sat fat / 36g carbs / 6.5g sugars
0.8g salt / 5.7g fibre / 7.2g protein

1. Preheat the oven to 200°C/400°F/Gas Mark 6. Add the oil to a roasting tin and place in the oven to heat for 3–4 minutes.

2. Add the cumin seeds, paprika, allspice, cinnamon and salt to a small bowl, and mix together well.

3. Add the chickpeas to the roasting tin, drizzle over the date syrup, sprinkle with the spice mix and stir together. Roast in the preheated oven for 15–20 minutes, stirring once, until brown and crusty.

4. Spoon into a bowl and leave to cool before eating. Store any leftovers in a plastic container or preserving jar in the refrigerator.

24

SMOKY HIT

This is a quick and economical snack to make and perfect for having on the go. For an extra smoky flavour, drizzle over some tahini when adding the date syrup.

FRUIT & NUT TRAIL MIX

Trail mix must be an all-time favourite snack, and this recipe is brimming with energy-boosting, fibre-rich fruit, nuts and seeds.

SERVES: 12	PREP: 10 MINS	COOK: NO COOKING

85 g/3 oz chopped ready-to-eat dried apricots

85 g/3 oz dried cranberries

85 g/3 oz roasted cashew nuts

85 g/3 oz shelled hazelnuts

85 g/3 oz shelled Brazil nuts, halved

85 g/3 oz flaked almonds

4 tbsp toasted pumpkin seeds

4 tbsp sunflower seeds

4 tbsp toasted pine nuts

1. Place all the ingredients in an airtight container, close the lid and shake several times. Shake the container before each opening, then re-seal. This mix will stay fresh for up to 2 weeks if tightly sealed.

per serving: 261 kcals / 20.6g fat
2.7g sat fat / 17g carbs / 9.8g sugars
trace salt / 3.6g fibre / 6.9g protein

CHEWY APRICOT & ALMOND ENERGY BARS

These flapjack-style, dairy-free energy bars are great for carrying with you for a healthy mid-morning snack.

MAKES: 15   PREP: 25 MINS, PLUS COOLING   COOK: 30 MINS

115 g/4 oz coconut oil

85 g/3 oz light muscovado sugar

60 g/2¼ oz almond butter, or other nut butter

1 dessert apple, cored and coarsely grated

150 g/5½ oz porridge oats

40 g/1½ oz brown rice flour

55 g/2 oz unblanched almonds, roughly chopped

40 g/1½ oz sunflower seeds

200 g/7 oz dried apricots, diced

per bar: 235 kcals / 14g fat
7.2g sat fat / 26.6g carbs / 14.6g sugars
trace salt / 3.5g fibre / 4.2g protein

1. Preheat the oven to 180°C/350°F/Gas Mark 4. Line a 20-cm/8-inch shallow square cake tin with non-stick baking paper.

2. Heat the oil and sugar in a medium-sized saucepan over a low heat until the oil has melted and the sugar is dissolved. Remove from the heat and stir in the almond butter, until melted.

3. Add the apple, oats, flour, almonds and sunflower seeds, and mix together well.

4. Spoon two thirds of the mixture into the prepared tin and press down firmly. Sprinkle over the apricots and press firmly into the base layer, then dot the remaining oat mixture over the top in a thin layer so that some of the apricots are still visible.

5. Bake in the preheated oven for about 25 minutes, until the top is golden brown. Remove from the oven and leave to cool in the tin until almost cold, then cut into 15 small rectangles. Leave to cool completely, then lift the bars out of the tin, using the paper. Separate the bars and pack into a plastic container. Store in the refrigerator for up to 3 days.

NO WHEAT

These tasty bars are wheat-free, but do check the oats carefully. Some brands may be contaminated with other wheat or gluten cereals during harvesting and milling.

SUPER SEEDY GRANOLA

Traditionally thought of as a breakfast cereal with milk, granola also makes a crunchy, sweet-tasting snack served on its own.

SERVES: 6   PREP: 20 MINS, PLUS COOLING   COOK: 30–35 MINS

150 g/5½ oz porridge oats
40 g/1½ oz pumpkin seeds
40 g/1½ oz sunflower seeds
40 g/1½ oz sesame seeds
1 tsp ground cinnamon
2 tbsp light muscovado sugar
2 tbsp olive oil
2 tbsp clear honey
juice of 1 small orange
40 g/1½ oz dried apple slices, diced
40 g/1½ oz dried blueberries
40 g/1½ oz dried cranberries

per serving: 358 kcals / 16.3g fat
2.2g sat fat / 48g carbs / 23.5g sugars
trace salt / 6.2g fibre / 12.3g protein

1. Preheat the oven to 160°C/325°F/Gas Mark 3. Add the oats, pumpkin seeds, sunflower seeds and sesame seeds to an 18 x 28-cm/7 x 11-inch roasting tin. Sprinkle with the cinnamon and sugar, and stir together.

2. Drizzle the oil, honey and orange juice over the top and mix together. Bake in the preheated oven for 30–35 minutes, stirring after 15 minutes, moving the mix in the corners to the centre as the edges brown more quickly. Try to keep the granola in clumps. Return to the oven and stir every 5–10 minutes, until the granola is an even, golden brown.

3. Scatter the dried apple, blueberries and cranberries over the top and leave the granola to cool and harden. Spoon into a plastic container or preserving jar and store in the refrigerator for up to 4 days.

MIX & MATCH

Vary the types of seeds or omit them and replace with your favourite nuts – unblanched, roughly chopped almonds or whole hazelnuts would work well.

2

TAKE TO WORK

. . . .

This chapter contains nutritious and filling
snacks that are ideal for taking to work –
and they'll keep you away from the vending
machine too!

ROASTED KALE CHIPS

Kale's flavour becomes wonderfully intense when the leaves are roasted. These chips are perfect on their own or sprinkled over soup.

SERVES: 4　　　**PREP: 20 MINS**　　　**COOK: 10–12 MINS**

250 g/9 oz kale
2 tbsp olive oil
2 pinches of sugar
2 pinches of sea salt
2 tbsp toasted flaked almonds,
to garnish

per serving: 122 kcals / 9.6g fat
1.1g sat fat / 8.1g carbs / 1.2g sugars
0.4g salt / 1.7g fibre / 3g protein

34

1. Preheat the oven to 150°C/300°F/Gas Mark 2. Remove the thick stems and central rib from the kale (leaving about 125 g/4½ oz trimmed leaves). Rinse and dry very thoroughly with kitchen paper. Tear into bite-sized pieces and place in a bowl with the oil and sugar, then toss well.

2. Spread about half the leaves in a single layer in a large roasting tin, spaced well apart. Sprinkle with a pinch of salt and roast on the bottom rack of the preheated oven for 4 minutes.

3. Stir the leaves, then turn the tray so the back is at the front. Roast for a further 1–2 minutes, until the leaves are crisp and very slightly browned at the edges. Repeat with the remaining leaves and salt. Sprinkle the kale chips with the flaked almonds to serve. These are best eaten on the day they are made.

TOP TIP

It's important to put the roasting tin on the bottom rack of the oven where the heat is gentler. The leaves can easily burn, so check them often.

RAINBOW NORI ROLLS

Brimming with protective antioxidants and vitamins, these colourful snacks can be filled with any combination of vegetables you like.

SERVES: 4   PREP: 30–35 MINS, PLUS COOLING   COOK: 27–30 MINS

175 g/6 oz sushi rice
750 ml/1¼ pints cold water
2 tbsp mirin
1 tbsp light olive oil
100 g/3½ oz asparagus tips
4 sheets nori
105 g/3¾ oz sliced sushi ginger, drained
25 g/1 oz kale, cut into thin strips
1 small red pepper, halved, deseeded and cut into thin strips
1 small yellow pepper, halved, deseeded and cut into thin strips
100 g/3½ oz carrots, cut into matchstick strips
100 g/3½ oz cooked beetroot in natural juices, drained and cut into matchstick strips
2 tbsp tamari
2 tbsp Chinese rice wine
sea salt

per serving: 235 kcals / 4.1g fat
0.5g sat fat / 41.6g carbs / 9g sugars
4.3g salt / 4.9g fibre / 6.2g protein

1. Put the rice and water into a saucepan with a little salt and bring to the boil, stirring occasionally. Reduce the heat and gently simmer for 18–20 minutes, until the rice is soft and has absorbed all the water. Stir occasionally towards the end of cooking so that the rice doesn't stick to the base of the pan. Remove from the heat and stir in the mirin. Leave to cool for 10 minutes.

2. Heat the oil in a frying pan, add the asparagus and fry over a medium heat for 3–4 minutes, until just soft, then set aside.

3. Separate the nori sheets and place one on a piece of clingfilm set on top of a bamboo sushi mat. Thinly spread one quarter of the warm rice over the top to cover the nori sheet completely.

4. Arrange one quarter of the ginger in an overlapping line a little up from one edge of the nori. Arrange one quarter of the asparagus and kale next to it, then one quarter of the red pepper and yellow pepper, then one quarter of the carrot and beetroot, leaving a border of rice about 2 cm/¾ inch wide.

5. Using the clingfilm and sushi mat, tightly roll the nori around the vegetables. Remove the bamboo mat, then twist the ends of the clingfilm and place the roll on a tray. Repeat to make three more nori rolls, then chill for 1 hour, or longer if preferred.

6. To serve, mix the tamari and rice wine together, then spoon into four small dipping bowls and set the bowls on serving plates. Unwrap each nori roll and cut into five thick slices. These are best eaten on the day they are made.

CHEESY FLAXSEED & QUINOA CRACKERS WITH TOMATO SALSA

These crackers are made with gluten-free quinoa flour and flaxseeds, so they're ideal for those on a wheat- or gluten-free diet.

SERVES: 4   **PREP: 35 MINS, PLUS COOLING**   **COOK: 12–15 MINS**

40 g/1½ oz golden flaxseeds, plus 1 tbsp for sprinkling

115 g/4 oz quinoa flour

½ tsp mustard powder

¼ tsp sea salt

pinch of cayenne pepper

55 g/2 oz butter, diced

55 g/2 oz mature Cheddar cheese, finely grated

2 eggs, 1 beaten, 1 separated

1 tbsp sesame seeds

SALSA

2 tomatoes, cut into wedges

1 spring onion, sliced

2–3 fresh coriander sprigs

sea salt and cayenne pepper

per serving: 378 kcals / 25.5g fat
11.5g sat fat / 24.3g carbs / 1.9g sugars
1.7g salt / 5.9g fibre / 13.7g protein

1. Preheat the oven to 190°C/375°F/Gas Mark 5. Grind 40 g/1½ oz of the flaxseeds in a spice mill to a coarse flour, then tip into a bowl and stir in the quinoa flour, mustard powder, salt and cayenne pepper.

2. Add the butter and rub in with your fingertips until the mixture resembles fine crumbs. Stir in the cheese, then mix in the egg and egg yolk, and press together with your hands to make a rough dough.

3. Gently knead the dough, then place between two sheets of non-stick baking paper, roll out to a rectangle and trim to 25 x 20 cm/10 x 8 inches. Cut into 2.5 x 10-cm/1 x 4-inch crackers. Leave the crackers on the paper and separate them slightly, then slide a baking sheet under the paper.

4. Lightly beat the egg white, then brush over the crackers and sprinkle with the remaining tablespoon of flaxseeds and the sesame seeds. Bake in the preheated oven for 12–15 minutes, until golden, then leave to cool on the paper.

5. Meanwhile, make the salsa by finely chopping the tomatoes, spring onion and coriander. Season with salt and cayenne pepper, and serve with the crackers. These are best eaten on the day they are made.

SUPER SEEDS

Flaxseeds, sometimes called linseeds, contain more minerals than any other seeds. Grinding or crushing them means the body is better able to absorb their nutrients.

COURGETTE & WALNUT ROLLS

It will be hard to resist the wonderful smell of these little rolls. Serve warm just as they are, with a little butter or soft goat's cheese.

MAKES: 8   PREP: 25 MINS, PLUS RISING   COOK: 10–12 MINS

olive oil, for oiling

450 g/1 lb mixed grain wholemeal flour, plus extra for dusting

1 tsp caraway seeds

1 tsp sea salt

2 tbsp dark molasses sugar

25 g/1 oz butter

2 tsp easy-blend dried yeast

200 g/7 oz courgettes, coarsely grated

150 ml/5 fl oz lukewarm water

55 g/2 oz walnut pieces, roughly chopped

per roll: 297 kcals / 9.9g fat
2.5g sat fat / 47.4g carbs / 4.2g sugars
trace salt / 7.1g fibre / 9.3g protein

1. Line two baking sheets with non-stick baking paper.

2. Put the flour, caraway seeds, salt, sugar and butter into a mixing bowl and rub in the butter until the mixture resembles fine crumbs. Stir in the yeast.

3. Mix in the courgettes, then add the warm water and mix to a soft dough. Turn out onto a lightly floured surface, add the walnuts and knead for 5 minutes, until the dough is smooth and elastic.

4. Cut the dough into 8 pieces, then place on the prepared baking sheets. Loosely cover the tops with a piece of oiled clingfilm and leave in a warm place for 45 minutes–1 hour, or until the dough has risen.

5. Meanwhile, preheat the oven to 220°C/425°F/Gas Mark 7. Remove the clingfilm, dust the tops of the rolls with a little flour and bake in the preheated oven for 10–12 minutes, until golden brown and the bread sounds hollow when tapped on the bottom. Turn out onto a wire rack to cool before serving. Once cooled, store leftover rolls in an airtight container and eat within 2–3 days.

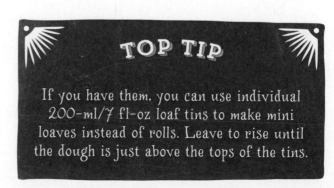

TOP TIP

If you have them, you can use individual 200-ml/7 fl-oz loaf tins to make mini loaves instead of rolls. Leave to rise until the dough is just above the tops of the tins.

GOAT'S CHEESE TRUFFLES WITH HONEY & PISTACHIO CRUMB

Made in no time at all, these tasty, high-protein savoury truffles are delicious served straight from the fridge.

MAKES: 12   PREP: 15 MINS, PLUS CHILLING   COOK: NO COOKING

150 g/5½ oz French rindless soft goat's cheese

1 tsp clear honey

40 g/1½ oz pistachio nuts, finely chopped

sea salt and pepper

per truffle: 54 kcals / 4.1g fat
2g sat fat / 1.5g carbs / 0.8g sugars
0.4g salt / 0.3g fibre / 3g protein

1. Mix the cheese and honey with a little salt and pepper in a bowl.

2. Scoop heaped teaspoons of the mixture onto a plate to make about 12 mounds.

3. Scatter the nuts over a separate, smaller plate, then roll one mound of cheese at a time in the nuts until evenly coated and shaped like a ball. Place on a plate and chill in the refrigerator for 1 hour before serving. Pack any leftover truffles into a small plastic container and store in the refrigerator for up to 3 days.

Take to work

PISTACHIOS

Pistachios are in fact seeds, not nuts, and come from a tree in the cashew family. Like most seeds, pistachios have an impressive fat profile, so watch your portion size to avoid clocking up the calories.

HONEY

Honey and, in particular, New Zealand Manuka honey has been shown to have potent antibacterial properties as well as an anti-inflammatory action that can quickly reduce pain once applied.

MEDJOOL DATES

Dates are a natural source of sweetness and make a great replacement for sugar. They also pack a nutritional punch, containing lots of fibre, potassium, manganese and vitamins A, B6 and K.

VINE TOMATOES

Tomatoes get their red colour from lycopene, a carotenoid pigment which, along with other antioxidants, may help protect against free-radical damage and prevent blood clots.

QUINOA

Native to Peru and Bolivia, this 'supergrain' is said to be the only plant food that contains all essential amino acids, putting it on a par with animal protein.

KALE

When in doubt, go for green! As well as containing high levels of vitamin C, folic acid and iron, the deep green pigment chlorophyll in green vegetables assists with the oxygenation and health of blood cells.

ROSEMARY, SEA SALT & SESAME POPCORN

Forget about fat- and additive-laden potato crisps – popcorn can be cooked in a fraction of the oil for a healthier alternative.

SERVES: 4　　　PREP: 10–15 MINS　　　COOK: 6–8 MINS

40 g/1½ oz sesame seeds

2 tbsp olive oil

2 rosemary stems, torn into large pieces

200 g/7 oz popping corn

1 tsp sea salt

2 tbsp balsamic vinegar, or to taste

per serving: 79 kcals / 25.2g fat
3.2g sat fat / 30g carbs / 1.6g sugars
1.5g salt / 6.6g fibre / 6.4g protein

1. Add the sesame seeds to a large frying pan with 1 teaspoon of the oil, cover and cook over a medium heat for 2–3 minutes, shaking the pan from time to time, until the seeds are toasted golden brown and beginning to pop. Scoop out of the pan into a bowl and wipe out the pan with a piece of kitchen paper.

2. Add the remaining oil and the rosemary to the pan and heat gently, shaking the pan to release the rosemary's oil. Add the corn, cover with the lid and cook over a medium heat for 3–4 minutes, shaking the pan, until all the popcorn has popped.

3. Remove from the heat and sprinkle with the toasted sesame seeds and season with the salt and vinegar, then tip into a serving bowl, discarding the rosemary just before eating.

GET POPPING

Popcorn is a natural wholegrain and a great source of complex carbohydrates. Stay away from the buttery and sugary toppings as these pile on the calories.

COCONUT, CACAO & HAZELNUT TRUFFLES

These little power-packed balls are just bursting with a nutritious mix of vital minerals, vitamins, protein and raw ingredients.

MAKES: 20   **PREP: 25 MINS**   **COOK: NO COOKING**

85 g/3 oz unblanched hazelnuts

55 g/2 oz cacao nibs, plus 1 tbsp for coating

6 dried 'soft' figs, roughly chopped

25 g/1 oz desiccated coconut, plus 2 tbsp for coating

1 tbsp maple syrup

finely grated rind and juice of ½ small orange

per truffle: 46 kcals / 3.5g fat
1g sat fat / 3.2g carbs / 2.1g sugars
trace salt / 0.9g fibre / 1.3g protein

1. Add the hazelnuts and the 55 g/2 oz cacao nibs to a food processor and process until very finely chopped.

2. Add the figs, the 25 g/1 oz coconut, maple syrup and orange rind and juice to the processor, and process until finely chopped and the mixture has come together in a ball.

3. Scoop the mixture out of the food processor, then cut into 20 even-sized pieces. Roll into small balls in your hands.

4. Finely chop the extra cacao nibs, then mix with the extra coconut on a sheet of non-stick baking paper or a plate. Roll the truffles, one at a time, in the cacao and coconut mixture, then arrange in a small plastic container. Store in the refrigerator for up to 3 days.

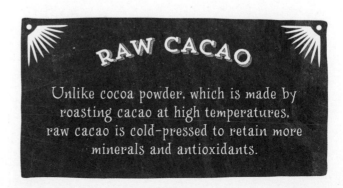

RAW CACAO

Unlike cocoa powder, which is made by roasting cacao at high temperatures, raw cacao is cold-pressed to retain more minerals and antioxidants.

WHOLEMEAL MUFFINS

These muffins are made with wholemeal flour and packed with fibre-rich fruit and oats – perfect for a treat.

MAKES: 10   PREP: 20–25 MINS, PLUS COOLING   COOK: 25–30 MINS

225 g/8 oz wholemeal flour
2 tsp baking powder
25 g/1 oz soft light brown sugar
100 g/3½ oz dried apricots, finely chopped
1 banana, mashed with 1 tbsp orange juice
1 tsp finely grated orange rind
300 ml/10 fl oz skimmed milk
1 egg, beaten
3 tbsp rapeseed or sunflower oil
2 tbsp porridge oats
honey or maple syrup, to serve (optional)

per muffin: 185 kcals / 5.5g fat
0.6g sat fat / 30.8g carbs / 11.1g sugars
0.7g salt / 3.7g fibre / 5.4g protein

1. Preheat the oven to 200°C/400°F/Gas Mark 6. Place 10 muffin cases in a muffin tin. Sift the flour and baking powder into a mixing bowl, adding any husks that remain in the sieve. Stir in the sugar and chopped apricots.

2. Make a well in the centre of the dry ingredients and add the banana, orange rind, milk, beaten egg and oil. Mix together well to form a thick batter. Divide the batter evenly between the 10 muffin cases.

3. Sprinkle each muffin with a few porridge oats and bake in the preheated oven for 25–30 minutes, or until well risen and firm to the touch. Transfer the muffins to a wire rack to cool slightly. Serve the muffins warm with a little honey or maple syrup, if using. Store the cooled muffins in an airtight plastic container for 2–3 days.

51

CHOCOLATE BROWNIE QUINOA COOKIES

Quinoa flour is made by grinding quinoa seeds and is a great grain- and gluten-free alternative to wheat flours.

MAKES: 26   PREP: 30 MINS, PLUS CHILLING   COOK: 12–14 MINS

55 g/2 oz coconut oil

100 g/3½ oz plain chocolate, 70% cocoa solids, broken into pieces

55 g/2 oz quinoa flour

1 tbsp cocoa powder

1 tsp bicarbonate of soda

½ tsp ground cinnamon

2 eggs

150 g/5½ oz light muscovado sugar

1 tsp natural vanilla extract

per cookie: 78 kcals / 4.3g fat
3g sat fat / 9.1g carbs / 7.1g sugars
trace salt / 0.7g fibre / 1.2g protein

1. Preheat the oven to 190°C/375°F/Gas Mark 5. Line three baking sheets with non-stick baking paper.

2. Place the oil and chocolate in a bowl and set over a saucepan of gently simmering water, making sure that the bowl is not touching the water. Heat for 5 minutes, or until the chocolate has melted, then stir to mix.

3. Add the quinoa flour, cocoa powder, bicarbonate of soda and cinnamon to a separate bowl and stir together.

4. Add the eggs, sugar and vanilla extract to a large mixing bowl and whisk together until thick and frothy. Gently fold in the oil and chocolate mixture, then add the flour mixture and stir until smooth.

5. Drop dessertspoons of the brownie mixture on the prepared trays, spaced well apart, then bake in the preheated oven for 7–9 minutes, until crusty and cracked, and still slightly soft to the touch. Leave to cool and harden slightly on the trays, then lift off the paper and pack into an airtight tin. Eat within 3 days.

53

RAW DATE & COCONUT BARS

These chunky, nutty bars get the most out of power-packed raw ingredients. Perfect to keep you energized at work all afternoon long.

MAKES: 12   PREP: 30 MINS, PLUS CHILLING   COOK: NO COOKING

400 g/14 oz medjool dates, halved and stoned

60 g/2¼ oz unblanched almonds

60 g/2¼ oz cashew nut pieces

35 g/1¼ oz chia seeds

2 tbsp maca (powdered superfood)

2 tsp natural vanilla extract

20 g/¾ oz desiccated coconut

55 g/2 oz unblanched hazelnuts, very roughly chopped

25 g/1 oz pecan nuts, broken in half

per bar: 225 kcals / 11g fat
2g sat fat / 31.7g carbs / 23.5g sugars
trace salt / 5.4g fibre / 4.2g protein

1. Add the dates, almonds and cashew pieces to a food processor and process until finely chopped

2. Add the chia seeds, maca and vanilla extract, and process until the mixture binds together in a rough ball.

3. Tear off two sheets of non-stick baking paper, put one on the work surface and sprinkle with half the coconut. Put the date ball on top then press into a roughly-shaped rectangle with your fingertips. Cover with the second sheet of paper and roll out to a 30 x 20-cm/12 x 8-inch rectangle. Lift off the top piece of paper, sprinkle with the remaining coconut, the hazelnuts and pecan nuts, then re-cover with the paper and briefly roll with a rolling pin to press the nuts into the date mixture.

4. Loosen the top paper, then transfer the date mixture, still on the base paper, to a tray and chill for 3 hours or overnight, until firm.

5. Remove the top paper, cut the date mixture into 12 pieces, peel off the base paper then pack into a plastic container, layering with pieces of baking paper to keep them separate. Store in the refrigerator for up to 3 days.

3

HIGH ENERGY

Part of leading a healthy, sustainable lifestyle
is regular exercise and these super-healthy
snacks are high in protein and healthy fats to
give you optimum amounts of energy.

APPLE & PEANUT BUTTER SANDWICHES

These fruity 'sandwiches' are the perfect pre-workout snack for lots of energy, minus the processed, wheat- and gluten-heavy bread.

SERVES: 4   PREP: 20 MINS   COOK: NO COOKING

2 green-skinned dessert apples
2 red-skinned dessert apples
juice of 2 lemons
115 g/4 oz crunchy peanut butter
4 tbsp dried cranberries, roughly chopped
2 tbsp sunflower seeds
2 tbsp porridge oats
60 g/2¼ oz dried apricots, diced
35 g/1¼ oz unblanched hazelnuts, roughly chopped

1. Cut each apple into six slices, then remove any pips (there is no need to core them). Put the apple pieces into a bowl, add the lemon juice and turn to coat evenly, to prevent discoloration.

2. Drain the apples, place on a tray or chopping board and spread each slice with peanut butter. Sprinkle half the slices with the cranberries, sunflower seeds, oats, apricots and hazelnuts.

3. Cover with the remaining apple slices, peanut butter-side downwards, and press together to make fruity sandwiches. Serve immediately.

per serving: 468 kcals / 23.4g fat
3g sat fat / 63.5g carbs / 43.1g sugars
trace salt / 10.7g fibre / 11g protein

AN APPLE A DAY

Apples are a good source of vitamin C and soluble pectin – the setting agent in jam – which is thought to help lower cholesterol and stimulate healthy gut bacteria.

PROTEIN BERRY WHIP

Frozen berries are a healthy and handy storecupboard staple. Blitz with protein-boosting cashew and Brazil nuts for a delicious shake.

SERVES: 4 PREP: 10–15 MINS COOK: NO COOKING

250 g/9 oz frozen mixed sliced strawberries and blueberries
40 g/1½ oz Brazil nuts
40 g/1½ oz cashew nut pieces
25 g/1 oz porridge oats
450 ml/16 fl oz almond milk
2 tbsp maple syrup

1. Place the frozen berries, Brazil nuts and cashew nuts in a blender. Sprinkle over the oats, then pour in half the almond milk. Blend until smooth.

2. Add the remaining milk and maple syrup, and blend again until smooth. Pour into four glasses and serve immediately with spoons. As the drink stands, the blueberries will almost set the liquid, but as soon as you stir it, it will turn to liquid again.

per serving: 213 kcals / 12.8g fat
2.4g sat fat / 23.2g carbs / 11.6g sugars
0.2g salt / 3.5g fibre / 4.7g protein

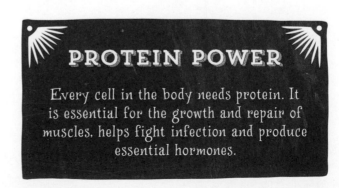

PROTEIN POWER

Every cell in the body needs protein. It is essential for the growth and repair of muscles, helps fight infection and produce essential hormones.

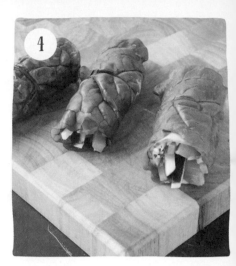

TURKEY & RAINBOW CHARD ROLL-UPS

Rainbow chard has the most beautiful pink, red, yellow or white stems and makes a nutritious alternative to kale.

MAKES: 8	PREP: 30 MINS	COOK: NO COOKING

8 rainbow chard leaves and stems (choose leaves that are about the same size as the slices of turkey)

1 avocado, halved and stoned

juice of 1 lemon

8 thin slices cooked turkey

150 g/5½ oz hummus

2 spring onions, trimmed and cut into very fine strips

1 carrot, cut into matchstick strips

100 g/3½ oz courgettes, cut into matchstick strips

per roll-up: 104 kcals / 6.1g fat
1g sat fat / 7.5g carbs / 1.6g sugars
0.5g salt / 3.6g fibre / 6.5g protein

1. Cut the stems from the chard leaves, then cut the stems into very thin matchstick strips and set aside. Peel the avocado and cut into long, thin slices, then toss in the lemon juice and set aside.

2. Separate the chard leaves and arrange, shiny-side down, on a large chopping board. Cover each one with a slice of turkey, then spread the turkey with a little hummus.

3. Divide the chard stems, spring onions, carrot and courgettes between the chard leaves, making a little pile on each leaf that runs in the centre of the leaf from long edge to long edge.

4. Top the little mounds with the avocado slices, then roll up from the base of the leaf to the tip and put on a plate, join downwards. Continue until all the leaves have been rolled.

5. Cut each roll into thick slices and transfer to individual plates, or wrap each roll in clingfilm and chill for up to 1 hour. Don't keep them for longer as the avocado will begin to discolour.

63

 EAT MORE VEG

Sneaking raw vegetables into energy-boosting snacks like this is the easiest way to increase your vitamin intake. Any combination of vegetables will do.

LOADED SWEET POTATOES

This veggy version of a jacket potato is topped with Middle-Eastern spiced chickpeas and tomatoes for a light but mighty refuelling snack.

SERVES: 4   PREP: 20–25 MINS   COOK: 50–55 MINS

4 small sweet potatoes, scrubbed
1 tbsp olive oil
1 small onion, chopped
1 garlic clove, finely chopped
1 tsp ground coriander
½ tsp ground cumin
200 g/7 oz tomatoes, peeled and diced
2 tsp tomato purée
200 g/7 oz canned chickpeas, drained
4 tbsp chopped fresh coriander
115 g/4 oz fat-free Greek-style yogurt
sea salt and pepper

per serving: 257 kcals / 4.2g fat
0.5g sat fat / 47.8g carbs / 9.8g sugars
0.9g salt / 8.1g fibre / 8.4g protein

1. Preheat the oven to 190°C/375°F/Gas Mark 5. Prick the potatoes with a fork, put them on a baking sheet and bake in the preheated oven for 45–50 minutes, or until they feel soft when squeezed.

2. Meanwhile, heat the oil in a small frying pan, add the onion and fry over a medium heat for 4–5 minutes, until soft. Stir in the garlic, ground coriander and cumin, and cook for a further minute.

3. Mix in the tomatoes, tomato purée and chickpeas, then season with a little salt and pepper. Cover and cook for 10 minutes, then remove from the heat and set aside.

4. Transfer the potatoes to a serving plate, slit each along its length and open out slightly. Reheat the chickpeas and spoon them over the potatoes. Mix half the fresh coriander into the yogurt and spoon over the chickpeas. Sprinkle with the remaining fresh coriander and serve immediately.

OPT FOR SWEET

Sweet potatoes are overflowing with the antioxidant beta-carotene, vitamin C and A, and their high fibre content will give you a great post-workout energy boost.

CHIPOTLE TURKEY CROQUETTES WITH PARMESAN & FLAXSEED CRUST

It might not look like a healthy snack, but these croquettes are baked rather than fried and the lean turkey is full of healthy minerals.

SERVES: 4   PREP: 35–40 MINS   COOK: 20–25 MINS

1–2 tbsp olive oil

4 spring onions, quartered

1 small red pepper, deseeded and cut into chunks

1 carrot, coarsely grated

2 tsp fresh thyme leaves

500 g/1 lb 2 oz fresh turkey breast mince

1 tsp mild paprika

1 small dried chipotle chilli, finely chopped

1 egg

1 tbsp cold water

25 g/1 oz freshly grated Parmesan cheese

55 g/2 oz golden flaxseeds, finely ground

sea salt and pepper

AVOCADO DIP

1 large ripe avocado, halved and stoned

grated zest and juice of 1 lime

2 tbsp fat-free Greek-style yogurt

per serving: 414 kcals / 22.4g fat
3.8g sat fat / 14.4g carbs / 3.4g sugars
1.2g salt / 8.9g fibre / 40.3g protein

1. Preheat the oven to 200°C/400°F/Gas Mark 6. Brush a baking sheet with a little of the oil. Finely chop the onions and red pepper in a food processor. Add the carrot, thyme and turkey, then sprinkle over the paprika, chilli and a little salt and pepper. Process until evenly mixed together.

2. Scoop out dessertspoons of the mixture onto a chopping board to make 16 oval-shaped mounds, then press them into neater shapes between your hands.

3. Lightly mix the egg, water and a little salt and pepper together in a shallow dish. Mix the cheese and flaxseeds in a separate shallow dish. Dip the croquettes, one at a time, into the egg, lift out with two forks, draining well, then roll in the cheese mixture. Place on the prepared baking sheet. Continue until all the croquettes are coated.

4. Bake in the preheated oven for 20–25 minutes, until golden, turning halfway through cooking and brushing with the remaining oil, if needed. To check that they are cooked, cut one croquette in half – the juices will run clear with no traces of pink.

5. When the croquettes are almost ready to serve, make the dip. Scoop the avocado from the shell, mash with the lime zest and juice, and mix with the yogurt. Spoon into a small bowl set on a large plate, then arrange the hot croquettes around the dish and serve immediately.

High energy

CHIA SEEDS

Chia-seeds were a staple crop among the Mayans and Aztecs, rumoured to be more valuable than gold, and for good reason – these tiny seeds are a nutritional powerhouse full of healthy fats and a host of potent antioxidants.

BLUEBERRIES

Blueberries are among the most powerful superfoods, with the same amount of antioxidants as five servings of other fruit and vegetables.

PEANUT BUTTER

Good quality peanut butter is an excellent source of protein and healthy monounsaturated fats, but be sure to choose organic, unsweetened varieties in order to maximize the health benefits.

GOJI BERRIES

These little red berries are rich in carotenes, which help to boost the immune system, and some research suggests that regular consumption can protect again heart disease and cancer.

OATS

Oats are a valuable source of whole grains, which help with reducing inflammation and maintaining a healthy weight. They are also very high in protein – equal to soya protein – and the hull-less oat kernel (the groat) is the highest of all cereals.

CHICKEN, KALE & CHIA SEED BITES

These bites may be small, but they clock up an impressive nutritional profile, with lean chicken, leafy kale and powerful chia seeds.

MAKES: 16   **PREP: 20–25 MINS, PLUS COOLING**   **COOK: 21 MINS**

2 x 125-g/4½ oz boneless, skinless chicken breasts

1 garlic clove, finely chopped

55 g/2 oz kale, shredded

115 g/4 oz light cream cheese

grated zest of 1 lemon, plus lemon wedges to serve

2 tsp chia seeds

sea salt and pepper

fresh chutney or pickle, to serve

per bite: 36 kcals / 1.6g fat
0.7g sat fat / 1.1g carbs / 0.4g sugars
0.3g salt / 0.2g fibre / 4.1g protein

1. Place the chicken breasts in the top of a steamer half-filled with boiling water. Sprinkle with the garlic, season with salt and pepper, cover with a lid and cook over a medium heat for 20 minutes, or until the juices run clear with no trace of pink when the chicken is pierced with a sharp knife.

2. Add the kale to the steamer and cook for 1 minute to soften it slightly.

3. Remove the steamer from the pan and leave to cool, then finely chop the chicken and kale.

4. Mix the cream cheese, lemon zest and chia seeds together, then stir in the chicken and kale. Taste and adjust the seasoning if needed.

5. Using two teaspoons, scoop spoonfuls of the mixture onto a plate, scraping off with the second spoon. Roll the mixture into balls, then pack into a plastic container. Seal and store in the refrigerator for up to 2 days. Serve with fresh chutney and lemon wedges.

LOVELY LEFTOVERS

This is a great way to use up leftover roast chicken. Begin the recipe at step 3 and add the cooked chicken to the cooled kale.

GINGER & OAT NO-BAKE BISCUITS

This is a low-sugar version of the beloved flapjack. Sweet, gingery and oaty, these biscuits have an irresistible flavour.

MAKES: 8   **PREP: 10–15 MINS, PLUS CHILLING**   **COOK: 8–10 MINS**

50 g/1¾ oz unsalted butter
200 ml/7 fl oz double cream
1 heaped tbsp unsweetened, smooth peanut butter
3 tbsp honey
1 tbsp ground ginger
200 g/7 oz large rolled oats

per biscuit: 175 kcals / 11.8g fat
6.3g sat fat / 14g carbs / 1.6g sugars
0.2g salt / 2g fibre / 3.8g protein

1. Put the butter, cream and peanut butter in a saucepan and bring to the boil over a medium heat, stirring from time to time. Turn the heat down to medium–low and cook for 5 minutes.

2. Tip all the remaining ingredients into the pan and stir to mix well.

3. Line a baking sheet with baking paper. Drop tablespoons of the mixture onto the tray, then cover and chill in the refrigerator for 25 minutes to harden before serving.

GOJI, MANGO & PISTACHIO POPCORN SLICES

This version of 'refrigerator cake' uses mineral-boosting dried fruit and seeds for a nutrient-dense, energy-packed treat.

MAKES: 12 **PREP: 25 MINS, PLUS CHILLING** **COOK: 6–8 MINS**

1 tbsp light olive oil

40 g/1½ oz popping corn

115 g/4 oz crunchy peanut butter

2 tbsp coconut oil

2 tbsp maple syrup

6 tbsp full-fat or semi-skimmed milk

100 g/3½ oz plain chocolate, 70% cocoa solids, broken into pieces

25 g/1 oz goji berries, roughly chopped

25 g/1 oz dried mango slices, finely chopped

25 g/1 oz pistachio nuts, roughly chopped

15 g/½ oz sunflower seeds

15 g/½ oz pumpkin seeds

per slice: 195 kcals / 13.8g fat
5.4g sat fat / 13.3g carbs / 7.5g sugars
0.1g salt / 2.2g fibre / 4.5g protein

74

1. Line a 20-cm/8-inch shallow square cake tin with a sheet of non-stick baking paper.

2. Heat the olive oil in a frying pan, then add the corn, cover with a lid and cook over a medium heat for 3–4 minutes, until all the corn has popped. Transfer to a bowl, discarding any grains that haven't popped, and wipe out the pan with kitchen paper.

3. Add the peanut butter, coconut oil, maple syrup and milk, and heat gently for 2–3 minutes, stirring until smooth. Remove from the heat, add the chocolate and set aside for 4–5 minutes, until the chocolate has melted.

4. Add the popcorn to the chocolate mix and lightly stir together. Tip into the prepared tin, press down flat with the back of a fork, then sprinkle with the goji berries, mango, pistachios, sunflower and pumpkin seeds. Press the topping into the soft chocolate mix, then chill in the refrigerator for 2 hours, until firmly set.

5. Lift the chocolate mixture out of the tin, place on a chopping board, peel away and reserve the paper, then cut the slice into 12 pieces. Pack into a plastic container, layering with the reserved paper. Keep in the refrigerator for up to 4 days.

CHOCOLATE & PEANUT BUTTER ENERGY BALLS

Very dark chocolate contains the same powerful antioxidant found in red wine and can positively influence a variety of health conditions.

MAKES: 8   PREP: 20–25 MINS, PLUS CHILLING   COOK: NO COOKING

50 g/1¾ oz blanched almonds

60 g/2¼ oz unsweetened peanut butter

20 g/¾ oz unsalted peanuts, roughly chopped

3 tbsp flaxseeds

30 g/1 oz plain chocolate with 85% cocoa, finely chopped

1 tsp cocoa powder

sea salt

per ball: 144 kcals / 11.9g fat
2.1g sat fat / 5.9g carbs / 1.7g sugars
0.3g salt / 3g fibre / 4.9g protein

1. Put the almonds in a food processor and process for a minute, until you have the texture of rough flour.

2. Put the peanut butter, peanuts, flaxseeds, chocolate and a small pinch of salt in a bowl, and mix. Add the almond flour, reserving 1½ tablespoons. Mix until you have a texture resembling chunky clay.

3. Sprinkle the remaining almond flour and the cocoa powder onto a plate and mix with a teaspoon. Form a tablespoon-sized blob of the peanut mixture into a ball using your palms. Roll it in the cocoa powder mixture, then transfer to a plate. Make a further seven balls in the same way.

4. Cover and chill in the refrigerator for at least 30 minutes before serving, or up to 2 days.

BANANA FLATBREAD BITES WITH TAHINI & DATE SYRUP

Sometimes the best things are the simplest. Assembled in minutes, this speedy snack is perfect for combating the 4 p.m. energy slump.

SERVES: 4   PREP: 15–20 MINS   COOK: 5–6 MINS

4 x 20-cm/8-inch wholemeal tortillas

4 tbsp tahini

3 tbsp date syrup

4 bananas, peeled

per serving: 354 kcals / 11.3g fat
2.5g sat fat / 60g carbs / 25.4g sugars
0.5g salt / 4.1g fibre / 9.4g protein

1. Preheat a dry frying pan, then add the tortillas, one by one, and warm for 30 seconds each side.

2. Arrange the tortillas on a chopping board, thinly spread each with the tahini, then drizzle with the date syrup. Add a whole banana to each tortilla, just a little off centre, then roll up tightly.

3. Cut each tortilla into thick slices, secure the bites with a cocktail stick and arrange on a plate. Serve warm.

GO BANANAS

Bananas are the only fruit to contain both tryptophan and vitamin B6, which produce serotonin – the natural chemical that helps lift your mood.

4

WEEKEND
SNACKS

Weekend snacks are inevitable, but even these
need not be processed and unhealthy with this
collection of tasty recipes – ideal for when you
have that little bit of extra time to prepare.

CHICKEN SATAY SKEWERS WITH PEANUT SAUCE

Chicken is one of the best sources of lean protein and unsweetened peanut butter contains lots of healthy monounsaturated fats.

SERVES: 4   PREP: 25–30 MINS, PLUS MARINATING   COOK: 6–8 MINS

4 skinless, boneless chicken breasts, about 115 g/4 oz each, cut into 2-cm/¾-inch cubes

4 tbsp soy sauce

1 tbsp cornflour

2 garlic cloves, finely chopped

2.5-cm/1-inch piece fresh ginger, peeled and finely chopped

1 cucumber, diced, to serve

PEANUT SAUCE

2 tbsp groundnut or vegetable oil

½ onion, finely chopped

1 garlic clove, finely chopped

4 tbsp unsweetened crunchy peanut butter

4–5 tbsp water

½ tsp chilli powder

per serving: 327 kcals / 16.8g fat
2.9g sat fat / 12.6g carbs / 3.7g sugars
2.4g salt / 2.2g fibre / 32.4g protein

1. Put the chicken cubes in a shallow dish. Mix the soy sauce, cornflour, garlic and ginger together in a small bowl and pour over the chicken. Cover and leave to marinate in the refrigerator for at least 2 hours.

2. Meanwhile, soak 12 wooden skewers in cold water for at least 30 minutes. Preheat the grill and thread the chicken pieces onto the wooden skewers. Transfer the skewers to a griddle pan and cook under a preheated grill for 3–4 minutes. Turn the skewers over and cook for a further 3–4 minutes, or until cooked through. To make sure the chicken is cooked, cut into the middle to check there are no remaining traces of pink or red.

3. Meanwhile, to make the sauce, heat the oil in a saucepan, add the onion and garlic, and cook over a medium heat, stirring frequently, for 3–4 minutes, until softened. Add the peanut butter, water and chilli powder and simmer for 2–3 minutes, until softened and thinned. Serve the skewers immediately with the warm sauce and cucumber.

KALE & GREEN GARLIC BRUSCHETTA

Green or 'wet' garlic is the garlic from the very first crop of the season. Soft and delicious, it is excellent spread on wholegrain toast.

SERVES: 4   PREP: 25 MINS   COOK: 25 MINS

1 green garlic bulb

3 tbsp olive oil

4 slices sourdough bread with mixed or sprouted seeds, total weight 250 g/9 oz

85 g/3 oz shredded kale, rinsed well and drained

1 tbsp balsamic vinegar

2 tsp pomegranate molasses

sea salt and pepper

per serving: 278 kcals / 12.7g fat
1.7g sat fat / 35.4g carbs / 3.6g sugars
1.4g salt / 4.8g fibre / 7.3g protein

1. Preheat the oven to 190°C/375°F/Gas Mark 5. Put the garlic bulb on a piece of foil, drizzle with 1 tablespoon of the oil, then wrap the foil around it and seal well. Put on a baking sheet and roast in the preheated oven for 20 minutes, or until the bulb feels soft when squeezed.

2. Meanwhile, preheat a ridged griddle pan. Cut the bread slices in half, brush one side of each with a little oil, then cook the bread, oiled-side down, in the hot pan for 2 minutes. Brush the top with the remaining oil, then turn and cook the second side until golden brown.

3. Unwrap the garlic, peel away the outer casing from the bulb, separate the cloves, then remove any of the tougher skins. Crush the creamy soft garlic to a coarse paste using a pestle and mortar. Mix the paste with any juices from the foil, then thinly spread on the griddled bread and keep warm.

4. Heat a dry, non-stick frying pan, add the kale and cook over a medium heat for 2–3 minutes, until just wilted. Mix in the vinegar, molasses and a little salt and pepper. Arrange the bruschetta on a chopping board, spoon over the kale and serve.

 GO GREEN

Green, leafy vegetables like kale, chard and cabbage are rich in iron and contain the pigment chlorophyll, which helps to increase the oxygenation of blood cells.

85

CHICKEN- AND CHEESE-STUFFED MINI PEPPERS

Filled with oozing cheese, these tasty little mouthfuls are perfect for serving as appetizers for a dinner party.

MAKES: 12   **PREP: 30–35 MINS**   **COOK: 15 MINS**

olive oil, for oiling

70 g/2½ oz full-fat cream cheese

2 garlic cloves, finely chopped

2 tsp finely chopped fresh rosemary

1 tbsp finely chopped fresh basil

1 tbsp finely chopped fresh parsley

15 g/½ oz finely grated Parmesan cheese

150 g/5½ oz cooked chicken breast, finely chopped

3 spring onions, finely chopped

12 mixed coloured baby peppers, about 350 g/12 oz total weight

sea salt and pepper

per stuffed pepper: 59 kcals / 3.2g fat
1.5g sat fat / 2.4g carbs / 1.7g sugars
0.4g salt / 0.7g fibre / 5g protein

86

1. Preheat the oven to 190°C/375°F/Gas Mark 5. Lightly brush a large baking sheet with oil.

2. Put the cream cheese, garlic, rosemary, basil and parsley in a bowl, then add the Parmesan and stir together with a metal spoon.

3. Mix in the chicken and spring onions, then season with a little salt and pepper.

4. Slit each pepper from the tip up to the stalk, leaving the stalk in place, then make a small cut just to the side, so that you can get a teaspoon into the centre of the pepper to scoop out the seeds.

5. Fill each pepper with some of the chicken mixture, then place on the prepared baking sheet. Cook in the preheated oven for 15 minutes, or until the peppers are soft and light brown in patches.

6. Leave to cool slightly on the baking sheet, then transfer to a serving plate. Serve warm or cold. These are best eaten on the day they are made and should be kept in the refrigerator if serving cold.

FLAVOUR TWIST

For a spicy, smoky twist, try adding 1/2 teaspoon chilli flakes and 1/2 teaspoon smoked paprika to the cheese mixture before stuffing the peppers.

BROAD BEAN & MINT HUMMUS WITH CRUDITÉS

This summery hummus, made with freshly podded broad beans flavoured with chopped garden herbs, is delicious on warm pittas.

SERVES: 4   PREP: 30–35 MINS   COOK: 15 MINS

350 g/12 oz podded broad beans
2 tbsp virgin olive oil
1 tsp cumin seeds, crushed
3 spring onions, thinly sliced
2 garlic cloves, finely chopped
25 g/1 oz fresh mint, torn into pieces
25 g/1 oz fresh flat-leaf parsley, finely chopped
juice of 1 lemon
60 g/2¼ oz Greek-style natural yogurt
sea salt and pepper

TO SERVE

1 red and 1 yellow pepper, deseeded and cut into strips
4 celery sticks, cut into strips
½ cucumber, halved, deseeded and cut into strips
1 portion of pittas, cut into strips (optional)

per serving: 446 kcals / 13.7g fat
2.5g sat fat / 67.7g carbs / 8.4g sugars
2.3g salt / 15.5g fibre / 19.1g protein

1. Half-fill the base of a steamer with water, bring to the boil, then put the broad beans in the steamer top, cover with a lid and steam for 10 minutes, or until tender.

2. Meanwhile, heat the oil in a frying pan over a medium heat. Add the cumin, spring onions and garlic, and cook for 2 minutes, or until the onion is softened.

3. Put the beans in a food processor or blender, add the onion mixture, herbs, lemon juice and yogurt and season with a little salt and pepper. Process to a coarse purée, then spoon into a dish set on a large plate.

4. Arrange the vegetable strips around the hummus and serve with the pittas, if using.

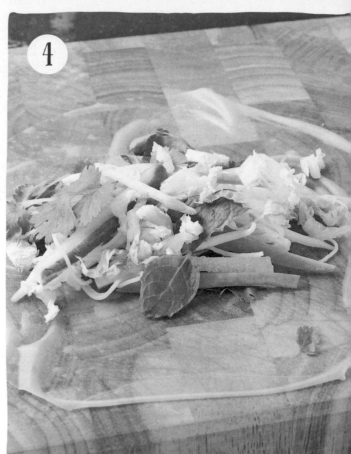

VIETNAMESE PRAWN RICE PAPER ROLLS

Wonderfully light, gluten-free and practically fat-free, these moreish snacks are full of protein-rich shellfish and crunchy raw vegetables.

MAKES: 6   PREP: 40 MINS   COOK: NO COOKING

40 g/1½ oz vermicelli rice noodles

150 g/5½ oz cooked and chilled tiger prawns, rinsed with cold water, drained and thickly sliced

grated zest of 1 lime

10 g/¼ oz fresh mint, leaves torn from stems

10 g/¼ oz fresh coriander, long stems trimmed

55 g/2 oz beansprouts, rinsed and drained

55 g/2 oz carrots, cut into matchstick strips

¼ cucumber, halved lengthways, deseeded and cut into matchstick strips

½ cos lettuce heart, leaves shredded

6 x 20-cm/8-inch rice spring roll wrappers

DIPPING SAUCE
juice of 1 lime

1 tbsp tamari

1 tbsp light muscovado sugar

1 tsp Thai fish sauce

1 red chilli, halved, deseeded and finely chopped

2 garlic cloves, finely chopped

2.5-cm/1-inch piece fresh ginger, scrubbed and finely grated

per roll: 112 kcals / 0.4g fat
trace sat fat / 22.2g carbs / 4.3g sugars
1.3g salt / 1.6g fibre / 5g protein

1. Add the noodles to a shallow dish, cover with just-boiled water, then leave to soften for 5 minutes.

2. Mix the prawns with the lime zest. Arrange the mint, coriander, beansprouts, carrot sticks, cucumber sticks and shredded lettuce in separate piles on a tray. Drain the noodles and tip into a dish.

3. Pour some just-boiled water into a large, shallow round dish then dip one of the rice wrappers into the water. Keep moving in the water for 10–15 seconds until soft and transparent, then lift out, draining well, and place on a chopping board.

4. Arrange a few prawns in a horizontal line in the centre of the rice wrapper, leaving a border of wrapper at either end. Top with some mint leaves and coriander sprigs, then add a few noodles and beansprouts. Add some carrot and cucumber, and a little lettuce. Roll up the bottom third of the rice wrapper over the filling, fold in the sides, then roll up tightly to form a sausage shape. Place on a plate.

5. Repeat with the remaining wrappers until you have 12 rolls.

6. To make the dip, add the lime juice to a small bowl, stir in the tamari, sugar and fish sauce, then add the chopped chilli, garlic and ginger, and stir.

7. Cut each roll in half and serve immediately with individual bowls of the dipping sauce. If planning to serve later, wrap each roll in clingfilm and chill in the refrigerator for up to 8 hours.

Weekend snacks

MINT

Mint has soothing, anesthetic properties and is effective at calming the stomach. Mint tea made simply by steeping the fresh leaves in boiling water is also a good cure for hiccups!

CHILLIES

Hot chillies do more than add a little spice to your meals – their heat is also great for boosting the metabolism, which can help with weight loss by increasing body temperature.

PECAN NUTS

Pecan nuts are packed with plant sterols, which are effective at lowering cholesterol. They also contain high levels of oleic acid, the healthy fat found in avocados and olives.

ALMOND MILK

More than being a substitute for dairy milk, almond and other nut milks are great for getting a little extra protein into your diet. Try to buy organic where possible, as this uses real almonds for sweetness instead of added sugar.

FIGS

Originating in Asia, figs have an illustrious history. They are high in natural sugars, which, like dates, make them perfect for adding a healthier dose of sweetness to any dish.

BAKED FIGS WITH GORGONZOLA

Made with baby figs, just melting Gorgonzola, delicate wild flower honey and crunchy wholegrain toast, this snack is quite heavenly.

SERVES: 4　　　**PREP: 15 MINS**　　　**COOK: 10 MINS**

1 mixed-grain demi baguette, cut into 8 x 2-cm/¾-inch thick slices (total weight 100 g/3½ oz)

8 small fresh figs

55 g/2 oz Gorgonzola cheese, rind removed, cut into 8 squares

4 tsp clear wild flower honey

per serving: 195 kcals / 5.2g fat 2.8g sat fat / 28g carbs / 16.1g sugars 0.7g salt / 4.2g fibre / 6.9g protein

1. Preheat the oven to 180°C/350°F/Gas Mark 4. Lightly toast the bread on both sides, then transfer to a small baking sheet.

2. Cut a cross in the top of each fig, lightly press a cube of cheese into each one, then place a fig on top of each slice of toast. Bake in the preheated oven for 5–6 minutes, until the figs are hot and the cheese is just melting.

3. Transfer to a plate or chopping board. Drizzle with honey and serve immediately.

94

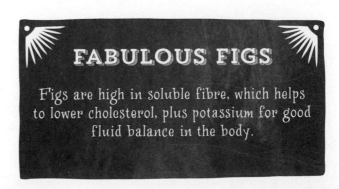

FABULOUS FIGS

Figs are high in soluble fibre, which helps to lower cholesterol, plus potassium for good fluid balance in the body.

APPLE & CINNAMON CRISPS

Crisp and crunchy, without the fat, salt and strong flavours of potato crisps, these make a much healthier alternative for all the family.

SERVES: 4   PREP: 20–25 MINS, PLUS COOLING   COOK: 1½–2 HRS

1 litre/1¾ pints water

1 tbsp sea salt

3 dessert apples, such as Braeburn or Gala

pinch of ground cinnamon

per serving: 72 kcals / 0.2g fat
trace sat fat / 19.1g carbs / 14.2g sugars
0.7g salt / 3.4g fibre / 0.3g protein

1. Preheat the oven to 110°C/225°F/Gas Mark ¼. Put the water and salt into a large mixing bowl and stir until the salt has dissolved.

2. Very thinly slice the apples, one at a time, with a sharp knife or mandolin, leaving the skin on and the core still in place, but removing any pips. Add each apple slice to the water. Turn to coat in the salt water, which will help prevent discolouration.

3. Drain the apple slices in a colander, then lightly pat dry with a clean tea towel. Arrange in a thin layer on a large cooking or roasting rack. Place this in the oven so that the heat can circulate under the slices as well as over the tops.

4. Bake for 1½–2 hours, until the apple slices are dry and crisp. Loosen with a palette knife and transfer to a large plate or chopping board, then sprinkle with cinnamon. Leave to cool completely, then serve or pack into a plastic container, seal and keep in the refrigerator for up to 2 days.

HOME-MADE CACAO & HAZELNUT BUTTER

This delicious nut butter, made with wholesome ingredients, is perfect spread on wholegrain toast or hot pancakes for a weekend treat.

MAKES: 225 g/8 oz   PREP: 15 MINS, PLUS STANDING   COOK: 3–4 MINS

115 g/4 oz unblanched hazelnuts
25 g/1 oz raw cacao powder
65 g/2½ oz light muscovado sugar
125 ml/4 fl oz light olive oil
½ tsp natural vanilla extract
pinch of sea salt
wholegrain toast or pancakes,
to serve (optional)

per 45g serving: 430 kcals / 40g fat
5.2g sat fat / 19.5g carbs / 13.9g sugars
0.3g salt / 4g fibre / 4.1g protein

1. Add the hazelnuts to a dry frying pan and cook over a medium heat for 3–4 minutes, constantly shaking the pan, until the nuts are an even golden brown in colour.

2. Wrap the nuts in a clean tea towel and rub to remove the skins.

3. Put the nuts into a blender and blend until finely ground. Add the cacao powder, sugar, oil, vanilla extract and salt, and blend again to make a smooth paste. Spoon into a small preserving jar and clip the lid in place. Leave to stand at room temperature for 4 hours, until the sugar has dissolved completely. Stir again, then store in the refrigerator for up to 5 days. Serve on wholegrain toast or hot pancakes, if using.

TOP TIP

Most nuts would work in this recipe – try replacing the hazelnuts with the same quantity of almonds for a tasty twist.

PUMPKIN & PECAN PANCAKES

Pancakes are the ultimate weekend treat and the addition of nuts and nutrient-rich pumpkin in this recipe gives them a healthy boost.

SERVES: 6   PREP: 20 MINS   COOK: 25–30 MINS

140 g/5 oz plain flour

20 g/¾ oz chopped pecan nuts

50 g/1¾ oz soft muscovado sugar

2 tsp baking powder

½ tsp cinnamon

¼ tsp sea salt

1 egg

300 ml/10 fl oz semi-skimmed buttermilk

200 g/7 oz peeled and cooked pumpkin, (prepared weight), mashed

1 tsp natural vanilla extract

vegetable oil spray

125 ml/4 fl oz honey or maple syrup, to serve

per serving: 246 kcals / 4.6g fat
1.1g sat fat / 45.2g carbs / 24.2g sugars
1.5g salt / 1.4g fibre / 6.1g protein

1. In a medium bowl, combine the flour, pecan nuts, sugar, baking powder, cinnamon and salt. In another large bowl, whisk the egg, buttermilk, pumpkin and vanilla extract. Whisk the dry ingredients into the wet ingredients and mix well.

2. Spray a non-stick frying pan with the vegetable oil spray and heat over a medium–high heat. When hot, ladle in the batter, 50 ml/2 fl oz at a time, to make 8–10-cm/3–4-inch pancakes.

3. Cook for about 2–3 minutes, or until bubbles begin to form on the surface and the base is lightly coloured. Flip over and cook for a further 2 minutes, or until the second side is lightly coloured. Serve immediately with honey.

ALMOND MILK-AND-COOKIE SHOTS

Refreshing almond milk served in a dark chocolate-lined, wholegrain hazelnut cookie – who said eating healthily was dull?

MAKES: 6   PREP: 35 MINS, PLUS CHILLING   COOK: 18–20 MINS

6 tbsp coconut oil, at room temperature, plus extra for oiling
55 g/2 oz light muscovado sugar
½ tsp natural vanilla extract
25 g/1 oz ground hazelnuts
25 g/1 oz ground golden flaxseeds
115 g/4 oz plain wholemeal flour
1 egg yolk
100 g/3½ oz plain chocolate, 70% cocoa solids
150 ml/5 fl oz unsweetened almond milk

per shot: 573 kcals / 39.7g fat
24.8g sat fat / 50.2g carbs / 21.4g sugars
trace salt / 8.2g fibre / 8.6g protein

1. Lightly grease 6 x 90-ml/3-fl oz dariole moulds and line each base with a round of non-stick baking paper.

2. Beat together the coconut oil, sugar and vanilla extract in a mixing bowl or food processor until light and creamy. Add the hazelnuts and flaxseeds, then add the flour and egg yolk, and beat together. Finely chop 30 g/1 oz of the chocolate and mix into the cookie crumbs. Using your hands, squeeze the dough into crumbly clumps.

3. Divide the mixture between the prepared moulds, then level with the back of a teaspoon. Transfer to a baking tray and chill in the refrigerator for 20 minutes. Meanwhile, preheat the oven to 180°C/350°F/Gas Mark 4.

4. Bake in the preheated oven for 13–15 minutes, until golden brown, then reshape the inside of the cups with the back of a small teaspoon. Leave to cool for 30 minutes.

5. Loosen the edges of the cups with a small, round-bladed knife and remove from the tin. Return to the tray and chill for at least 1 hour, until firmly set.

6. Break the remaining chocolate into a bowl set over a saucepan of very gently simmering water and heat until melted. Add spoonfuls of melted chocolate to the cookie cups, tilting to evenly cover the insides with chocolate. Chill for at least 30 minutes. When ready to serve, pour in the almond milk and serve on small saucers.

5

SWEET INDULGENCE

· ·

The best part about eating healthy, whole foods is that even sweets aren't off-limits if you're doing it right. This chapter contains lots of ideas for healthier sweet snacks for when the cravings kick in.

CHOCOLATE & MACADAMIA 'CUPCAKES'

These delicious mouthfuls are a hybrid between a cupcake and a cookie, and make a nutty and moreish wholesome treat.

MAKES: 12   PREP: 30 MINS, PLUS COOLING   COOK: 20 MINS

85 g/3 oz butter, at room temperature
85 g/3 oz crunchy peanut butter
85 g/3 oz light muscovado sugar
2 eggs, beaten
115 g/4 oz wholemeal flour
1 tsp baking powder
55 g/2 oz macadamia nuts, roughly chopped, plus 12 whole nuts to decorate (optional)

CHOCOLATE FROSTING
100 g/3½ oz plain chocolate, 70% cocoa solids, broken into pieces
25 g/1 oz butter, diced
25 g/1 oz light muscovado sugar
4 tbsp milk

per cupcake: 274 kcals / 19.2g fat
8.3g sat fat / 22.3g carbs / 12.3g sugars
0.5g salt / 2.9g fibre / 5.4g protein

1. Preheat the oven to 180°C/350°F/Gas Mark 4. Line a 12-hole muffin tin with paper cases.

2. Add the butter, peanut butter and sugar to a large bowl or food processor and beat together until light and fluffy.

3. Gradually beat a little of the egg into the butter mixture, alternating with a few spoonfuls of the flour, then continue until all the egg and flour have been added and the mixture is smooth. Beat in the baking powder and chopped nuts.

4. Divide the mixture between the paper cases, bake in the preheated oven for 15 minutes, until risen, golden brown and the tops spring back when lightly pressed with a fingertip. Leave to cool in the tins for 10 minutes.

5. To make the frosting, put the chocolate, butter, sugar and milk into a bowl set over a saucepan of gently simmering water and heat, stirring occasionally, for about 5 minutes, until smooth.

6. Spoon the frosting over the cakes to cover them completely, then top each with a macadamia nut, if using. Leave in a cool place for 30 minutes to cool completely. Remove from the tin and serve, or store any leftovers in a plastic container in the refrigerator for up to 1 day.

STRAWBERRY & PASSION FRUIT YOGURTS

If you fancy a light, sweet-tasting snack, these little jars of summery freshness will give you an instant boost.

SERVES: 4   PREP: 20–25 MINS, PLUS COOLING   COOK: 2–3 MINS

20 g/¾ oz desiccated coconut

200 g/7 oz strawberries, hulled

finely grated zest and juice of 1 lime

350 g/12 oz fat-free Greek-style yogurt

4 tsp clear honey

2 passion fruit, halved

1 tbsp dried goji berries, roughly chopped

per serving: 141 kcals / 3.5g fat
2.8g sat fat / 19.3g carbs / 14.6g sugars
trace salt / 3.2g fibre / 10.4g protein

1. Add the coconut to a dry frying pan and cook over a medium heat for 2–3 minutes, shaking the pan, until light golden in colour. Remove from the heat and leave to cool.

2. Roughly mash the strawberries and mix with half the lime juice.

3. Add the lime zest, remaining lime juice, the yogurt and honey to a bowl, and stir together. Add three quarters of the cooled coconut to the yogurt, then scoop the seeds from the passion fruit over the top and lightly fold into the yogurt.

4. Layer alternate spoonfuls of strawberry and yogurt in 4 x 200-ml/7-fl oz preserving jars, then sprinkle with the remaining coconut and the goji berries. Clip down the lids and chill until ready to serve. Eat within 24 hours.

RUBY FRUIT JUICE

There's nothing more refreshing than a locally grown strawberry in the summer, but this smoothie can be enjoyed at any time of year.

SERVES: 1   PREP: 15 MINS   COOK: NO COOKING

1 ruby red grapefruit, zest and a little pith removed, deseeded and roughly chopped

¼ cucumber, roughly chopped

150 g/5½ oz strawberries, hulled

small handful of crushed ice (optional)

1. Put the grapefruit and cucumber in a blender and blend until smooth.

2. Add the strawberries and crushed ice (if using) and blend again until combined.

3. Pour into a glass and serve immediately.

110

per serving: 162 kcals / 0.8g fat
trace sat fat / 40.4g carbs / 25.5g sugars
trace salt / 7.3g fibre / 3.4g protein

BLACK BEAN BROWNIES

Don't let on that these gluten-free brownies are made with black beans and dates until everyone is clamouring for seconds!

MAKES: 16   PREP: 25 MINS, PLUS COOLING   COOK: 28 MINS

100 g/3½ oz plain chocolate chips, 70% cocoa solids

3 tbsp coconut oil

375 g/13 oz black beans in water, drained

175 g/6 oz medjool dates, halved and stoned

3 eggs

70 g/2½ oz light muscovado sugar

1 tsp natural vanilla extract

55 g/2 oz cocoa powder

1½ tsp baking powder

½ tsp ground cinnamon

¼ tsp sea salt

per brownie: 139 kcals / 6.8g fat
4.4g sat fat / 17.6g carbs / 12.3g sugars
0.4g salt / 4g fibre / 3.7g protein

1. Preheat the oven to 180°C/350°F/Gas Mark 4. Line a 20-cm/8-inch shallow square cake tin with a square of non-stick baking paper.

2. Add 55 g/2 oz of the chocolate chips to a small saucepan with the oil and heat over a very low heat until the oil has melted, then remove and leave to stand for a few minutes until the chocolate has melted completely.

3. Meanwhile, add the beans and dates to a food processor or blender and process to a coarse purée. Add the eggs, sugar, vanilla extract, chocolate and coconut oil mixture, and process again until smooth.

4. Mix the cocoa powder, baking powder, cinnamon and salt together, then add to the bean mixture and process briefly until smooth.

5. Spoon into the prepared tin and spread in an even layer. Bake in the preheated oven for about 25 minutes, or until the cake is well risen, beginning to crack around the edges and still slightly soft in the centre.

6. Sprinkle with the remaining chocolate chips and leave to cool for 20 minutes. Lift the paper and brownies out of the tin and transfer to a wire rack to cool completely. Cut into 16 small pieces, lift off the paper and store in a tin for up to 2 days.

COCONUT MILK, STRAWBERRY & HONEY ICE CREAM

Everyone loves ice cream but it can be loaded with lots of sugar. This version is made with just three wholesome ingredients.

SERVES: 6   PREP: 30 MINS, PLUS FREEZING   COOK: NO COOKING

450 g/1 lb strawberries, hulled and halved

400 ml/14 fl oz canned full-fat coconut milk

85 g/3 oz clear honey

crushed hazelnuts, to serve (optional)

per serving: 198 kcals / 14.4g fat 12.6g sat fat / 19.3g carbs / 16.7g sugars trace salt / 1.8g fibre / 1.4g protein

1. Purée the strawberries in a food processor or liquidizer, then press through a sieve set over a mixing bowl to remove the seeds.

2. Add the coconut milk and honey to the strawberry purée and whisk together.

3. Pour the mixture into a large roasting tin to a depth of 2 cm/¾ inch, cover the top of the tin with clingfilm, then freeze for about 2 hours until just set.

4. Scoop back into the food processor or liquidizer and blitz again until smooth to break down the ice crystals. Pour into a plastic container or 900-g/2-lb loaf tin lined with non-stick baking paper. Place the lid on the plastic container or fold the paper over the ice cream in the loaf tin. Return to the freezer for 3–4 hours, or until firm enough to scoop.

5. Serve immediately or leave in the freezer overnight or until needed. Thaw at room temperature for 15 minutes to soften slightly, then scoop into individual dishes and top with crushed hazelnuts to serve, if using.

Sweet indulgence

STRAWBERRIES

Strawberries have been popular since the Roman times and are native to many parts of the world. Like many other fruits, strawberries were historically considered a luxury item only enjoyed by royalty.

PINK GRAPEFRUIT

Grapefruit has long been hailed as a diet food because of its nutritional profile being low in calories and high in phytonutrients. It's popping with vitamin C too, with a mere half a grapefruit meeting 78% of your daily vitamin C requirement.

PASSION FRUIT

As well as adding a sweet tang to a dessert, passion fruit pulp is also a good source of potassium, making it useful for lowering blood pressure.

COCONUT

Coconut boasts an array of health benefits, mostly due to its high levels of lauric acid, an anti-fungal, anti-viral 'miracle' ingredient, which is great for boosting the immune system.

DARK CHOCOLATE

Dark chocolate and, particularly, raw cacao, has been shown to have many health benefits, including protecting the nervous system. Choose chocolate with 70% cocoa solids or higher to ensure a minimal sugar content.

SUPERFOOD CHOCOLATE BARK

The darker the chocolate, the less sugar and more cocoa butter it contains, so always choose chocolate with at least 70% cocoa solids.

SERVES: 6   **PREP: 20 MINS, PLUS SETTING**   **COOK: 5 MINS**

100 g/3½ oz plain chocolate, 70% cocoa solids, broken into pieces

85 g/3 oz mixed Brazil nuts, unblanched almonds and pistachio nuts, roughly chopped

2 tbsp dried goji berries, roughly chopped

2 tbsp dried cranberries, roughly chopped

1 tbsp chia seeds

per serving: 227 kcals / 15.7g fat
5.3g sat fat / 17.7g carbs / 10.2g sugars
trace salt / 5.1g fibre / 5.1g protein

1. Place the chocolate in a bowl set over a saucepan of gently simmering water and heat for 5 minutes, until melted, making sure that the base of the bowl is not touching the water.

2. Line a large baking sheet with non-stick baking paper. Stir the chocolate, then pour it onto the paper and spread to a 20 x 30-cm/8 x 12-inch rectangle.

3. Sprinkle the nuts, berries and chia seeds over the top, then leave to set in a cool place or the refrigerator.

4. To serve, lift the chocolate off the paper and break into rough-shaped shards. Store in a plastic container in the refrigerator for up to 3 days.

118

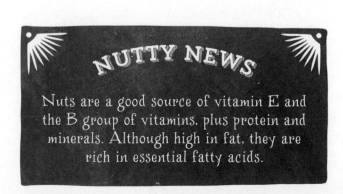

NUTTY NEWS

Nuts are a good source of vitamin E and the B group of vitamins, plus protein and minerals. Although high in fat, they are rich in essential fatty acids.

MINI ROASTED PEACH & RASPBERRY BLINIS

These dainty Russian pancakes make the perfect light treat. In the time it takes to make them, the roasted fruit topping will be ready.

MAKES: 20   PREP: 30 MINS   COOK: 30–40 MINS

4 small peaches, halved, stoned and cut into chunks
1 tbsp maple syrup
2 tbsp water
150 g/5½ oz raspberries
150 g/5½ oz full-fat crème fraîche
1 tsp natural vanilla extract

BLINI BATTER
85 g/3 oz buckwheat flour
1 tsp baking powder
1 egg
125 ml/4 fl oz semi-skimmed milk
1 tbsp light olive oil, for frying
sea salt

per blini: 59 kcals / 2.7g fat
1.1g sat fat / 7.6g carbs / 3.8g sugars
0.3g salt / 1.3g fibre / 1.6g protein

1. Preheat the oven to 190°C/375°F/Gas Mark 5. Place the peaches in a small roasting tin, drizzle over the maple syrup and water, then roast in the preheated oven for 10 minutes, until soft and just beginning to brown around the edges. Remove from the oven, sprinkle the raspberries into the hot tin and set aside.

2. Mix the crème fraîche with the vanilla extract and set aside.

3. To make the blinis, put the flour, baking powder and a pinch of salt into a bowl, and stir together. Add the egg, then gradually whisk in the milk until smooth.

4. Heat the oil in a large frying pan, then pour out the excess into a small bowl. Drop dessertspoons of the batter over the base of the pan, leaving a little space between each. Cook over a medium heat for 2–3 minutes, until bubbles begin to show on the surface and the undersides are golden brown. Turn over with a palette knife and cook for a further 1–2 minutes.

5. Lift the blinis out of the pan with a palette knife and keep warm in a clean tea towel. Heat the reserved oil in the pan, pour out the excess, then continue cooking the blinis in batches until all the batter has been used up.

6. Layer the blinis on a large plate with the crème fraîche and warm fruit, and serve immediately.

CHOCOLATE & AVOCADO PUDDING POTS

Unlike traditional chocolate mousses, this version doesn't need to be chilled and can be served just minutes after making.

MAKES: 4　　　PREP: 20 MINS　　　COOK: 5 MINS

55 g/2 oz plain chocolate, 70% cocoa solids, broken into pieces

1 large ripe avocado, halved and stoned

4 tbsp canned full-fat coconut milk

4 tsp maple syrup

½ tsp natural vanilla extract

pinch of sea salt

grated plain chocolate and lightly toasted coconut chips, to decorate (optional)

per pot: 246 kcals / 16.4g fat
7.3g sat fat / 24.5g carbs / 16.1g sugars
0.4g salt / 4.9g fibre / 2.4g protein

1. Place the chocolate in a bowl set over a saucepan of gently simmering water and heat for 5 minutes, making sure that the water doesn't touch the base of the bowl.

2. Scoop the avocado flesh from the skin into a food processor. Process until smooth, then add the coconut milk, maple syrup, vanilla extract and salt. Spoon in the melted chocolate and process until smooth.

3. Spoon the mixture into small shot glasses. Decorate the tops with a little grated chocolate and a few toasted coconut chips, if using. Serve immediately or chill in the refrigerator until needed.

HEALTHY FATS

Avocados have a bad press for being high in calories, but they are rich in healthy monounsaturated fat – the good kind that helps maintain healthy cholesterol levels.

RHUBARB & LEMON DRIZZLE SQUARES

Sometimes you just need a piece of cake – this healthier brown rice flour and almond cake is perfect for an afternoon pick-me-up.

- -

MAKES: 9   PREP: 30–35 MINS, PLUS COOLING   COOK: 35–40 MINS

300 g/10½ oz trimmed young rhubarb, cut into 2-cm/¾-inch thick slices
100 g/3½ oz ground almonds
115 g/4 oz brown rice flour
1½ tsp baking powder
1 ripe banana, mashed
150 ml/5 fl oz rice bran oil
115 g/4 oz light muscovado sugar
grated zest of 1 lemon
3 eggs
25 g/1 oz unblanched almonds, roughly chopped

SYRUP
juice of 2 lemons
60 g/2¼ oz light muscovado sugar

per square: 400 kcals / 26.1g fat
4.5g sat fat / 37.7g carbs / 22.6g sugars
0.6g salt / 3.2g fibre / 6.8g protein

1. Preheat the oven to 180°C/350°F/Gas Mark 4. Line a 30 x 20 x 4-cm/12 x 8 x 1½-inch square cake tin with a large piece of non-stick baking paper.

2. Place the rhubarb in a dry roasting tin and bake in the preheated oven for 10 minutes, until almost soft. Remove from the oven but do not switch the oven off.

3. Put the ground almonds, flour and baking powder into a bowl and stir together.

4. Put the banana, oil, sugar and lemon zest into a separate bowl and whisk together until smooth. Whisk in the eggs, one at a time, then beat in the flour mixture.

5. Spoon the batter into the prepared tin, then scatter the rhubarb over the top. Bake for 25–30 minutes, until the cake is well risen and the sponge springs back when pressed with a fingertip.

6. To make the syrup, mix the lemon juice with the sugar. Spoon half over the hot cake and leave to soak in for 1–2 minutes. Spoon over the remaining syrup, scatter with the chopped almonds and leave to cool in the tin.

7. Lift the cake out of the tin, peel away the paper and cut into 9 small pieces. Eat within 2 days or freeze until needed.

FROZEN YOGURT–COATED BERRIES

These look like sweets but they are bursting with fruity freshness, vitamin C and calcium. Keep a handy supply in the freezer.

SERVES: 4   PREP: 20–25 MINS, PLUS FREEZING   COOK: NO COOKING

225 g/8 oz fat-free Greek-style yogurt
1 tbsp clear honey
¼ tsp natural vanilla extract
115 g/4 oz blueberries
125 g/4¼ oz raspberries

per serving: 81 kcals / 0.3g fat
trace sat fat / 14.5g carbs / 10.8g sugars
trace salt / 2.7g fibre / 6.4g protein

1. Line three baking sheets or trays with non-stick baking paper, checking first that they will fit into your freezer.

2. Place the yogurt, honey and vanilla extract in a medium-sized bowl and stir together. Drop a few blueberries into the yogurt, then use two forks to coat the berries in a thin layer of yogurt. Lift out, one berry at a time, draining off the excess yogurt, and transfer to one of the lined trays.

3. Continue dipping and coating until all the blueberries are on the tray. Repeat with the raspberries. Freeze, uncovered, for 2–3 hours, until frozen hard.

4. Lift the berries from the trays and pack into polythene bags or lidded plastic containers. Seal and freeze for up to 1 month.

5. Remove as many as you need from the freezer and leave to thaw for 10 minutes before serving so that the fruit can soften slightly.

INDEX